Faith Walkers

Passages of Suffering and Hope

by
Joe Nassal, CPPS

PAULIST PRESS
New York and Mahwah, N.J.

Cover design by Tim McKeen.
Interior art by Cindy Gaudreau.

Library of Congress Cataloging-in-Publication Data

Nassal, Joe, 1955-
    Faith walkers : passages of suffering and hope
        p.   cm.
    ISBN 0-8091-3627-9 (alk. paper)
    1. Stations of the Cross—Meditations.   2. Spiritual life—Catholic Church.   3. Catholic Church—Doctrines.   I. Title.
BX2040.N37   1995   95-32125
232.96—dc20   CIP

Published by Paulist Press
997 Macarthur Boulevard
Mahwah, New Jersey 07430

Printed and bound in the United States of America

CONTENTS

For my mother,
Doris Nassal.
A woman who has
carried the cross,
making faith,
hope,
and love
contagious.

Introduction: A Journey of the Soul

We walk by faith, not by sight.
2 Cor. 5:7

The way of the cross is a sojourn of the soul.
This journey invites us to engage our imaginations
in a process of holy recovery—recovering the last steps
Jesus took on his walk on earth.
As such, this journey takes us to places we'd rather not go.
But by walking this way with Jesus,
we learn how not to become frustrated when fear and failure
creeps and seeps into our souls.
The *Way of the Cross* teaches us that we are
faithwalkers and not sightseers:
"we walk by faith and not by sight."
We are pilgrims not tourists.
The only postcards we purchase are from the edge
of time and space,
that place where heaven meets earth
and hope is born again and again.
The *Way of the Cross* has long been a popular devotion for
Christians, especially during Lent.
Catholic churches have placed these *Stations*
on their walls for centuries.
More than a pious devotion,
the *Way of the Cross* is a spiritual journey
that takes us across the treacherous terrain of the heart land;
beyond the grave to an eternal space where dreams are
conceived.
As we walk this way, be prepared to stop often.

Not to rest but to sense how this cross
is crushing our shoulders;
how the pebbles feel like boulders upon our bare feet;
how the splinters from the wood slice through our skin
and sink deep beneath the surface
to leave scars on our souls.
There are no exit ramps,
no rest stops,
along this harrowing yet holy way.
Winter's cold winds, ice, and snow have wounded
the pavement beneath our feet.
We will fall into potholes so large we will think
we will lose our lives if we are not careful.
But then, that's the point: be careful.
Be full of care for those who walk this way with us.
And when we are full
of such compassion and empathy
for those we meet along this way—
the weary ones,
the weeping ones,
the angry ones,
the violent ones,
the jeering ones,
the curious ones—
we will lose our lives.
And maybe, just maybe, find our souls.

■

We steady ourselves for this terrifying trip
that will have its tender moments
by reflecting on a modern psalm:

PSALM OF THE SOUL'S GREAT ESCAPE

Incarcerated in a bruised body
like a soldier in a prison camp,
the soul plots a great escape.
In the darkness after bed check
the soul's strategy takes shape.

The soul knows there is no sense
trying to go over the fence;
the barbed wire will slice the soul
into tiny bits of blood and tears.

The lights from the watchtower
will capture the soul's attempt
and while the soul hangs shredded
on the thorns above the fence,
the guns of the guards will finish
the soul's feeble bid to flee.

No, soul knows where it must go
to escape this prison of pain.
The soul must go deeper,
burrow down, under ground.
It will take more time but then,
when the soul's imprisoned,
time is an ally
not an acquaintance.

When we take time to dig beneath the surface of the soul's
discontent we discover the plan of salvation.
Rather than launching an air strike from above
to rescue humanity imprisoned in greed and selfishness,
sin and deceit,

God chose to stand in the prison of our pain with us.
God decided that an air strike to free the prisoners would cause
too much collateral damage and too many casualties.
Recognizing the first casualty in the war
between good and evil is truth,
God sent the truth to set us free.
Remember the scene:
Jesus stands before the powers-that-be and says,
The reason I was born,
the reason why I came into the world,
is to testify to the truth.
Anyone committed to the truth hears my voice. [John 18:37]
But Pilate doesn't understand.
"Truth!" he shouts. "What does that mean?" [v.18]
We have been asking the same question ever since.
What is truth?
Though we believe that whatever it is, it will set us free,
many of us fall into the same trap that Pilate did.
The truth stands before us in the people we will meet
along the road
but when faced with the responsibility to give witness
to this Truth,
we will be tempted to walk another way.
And we will live a lie.
So part of the reason we embark on this way of the cross
is to discover again not only the meaning of truth
but how we can give witness to this truth with our lives.
The truth is that God has come to the world
as the "Word made flesh."
In the Word, Jesus, God spoke once
and for all time and all peoples.
Remember what the beginning of the book of Hebrews says:

In times past,
God spoke in fragmentary and varied ways
to our ancestors through the prophets;
in this, the final age,
God has spoken to us through the Son,
whom God has made heir of all things
and through whom God created the universe. [Hebrews 1:1-2]
God's Word has been spoken:
a Word that shouts good news to the poor;
a Word that whispers consolation to the dying;
a Word that offers comfort to the grieving;
a Word that reflects light to those who live in darkness;
a Word that releases those who are imprisoned
behind bars of blame
and in maximum-security cells of shame;
a Word that breathes new hope in fearful hearts;
a Word that speaks truth to those who live a lie.
If we have the courage to walk this way,
live this truth,
embrace this life,
then we too will stand before the Pilates of our world
to testify.
We will be asked to place our hearts on this Word
and give voice to what our souls know:
we will tell the truth,
the whole truth,
and nothing but the truth.
And our prayer becomes:
"so help us God."
And we will tell it with our lives not with our lies.
We will tell it with acts of compassion not carelessness.
We will tell it to friends and enemies alike.

We will tell it tenaciously, yet tenderly;
poignantly yet powerfully.
Yes, we will tell it because we believe it.
Though we stumble now and again, we dare to walk this way,
live this truth,
discover this life
that awaits us.

■

We are aware that this journey of the soul will be stifled
by a sense of incompleteness,
and yet we choose to walk this way of the cross
because we believe that new insights into our own faith journey
might be found along the way.
Insight into ourselves:
our hearts, our minds, our bodies, our souls.
As we begin, remember this road sign.
It comes from a friend who saw it on the bulletin board
of a college Campus Ministry office:
"Religion is for those people who are afraid of going to hell;
Spirituality is for those who have been there."
This sign, penned by a college student,
gives us some direction for the journey before us.
By the end of this trip,
we will have the ashes and scars to show where we have been:
to hell and back again.
That is why this way of the cross
is not for the faint of heart.
It is not a stroll through pious fields
but through a spiritual valley of tears and fears.
If we have joined this pilgrimage to deepen our piety
or increase our devotion to the Stations of the Cross,

we will be disappointed.
But if we have embarked on this journey because we believe
that when the Word was made flesh,
God became incarnate in all the experiences of our lives,
then we are in the right place for this spiritual sojourn.
Then we know we walk by faith, not by sight.
We are faith walkers, not sight seers.
Steady your pilgrim hearts then,
for we are ready to begin.

OPENING PRAYER

Author of all Life, show us the Way;
teach us the Truth.
With your steady hand,
sign your name on our fragile faith
to give us the courage to walk with wisdom,
to act with compassion,
to speak with sincerity.
As we walk,
open our eyes that we might see you;
unstop our ears that we might hear your voice;
shred our hearts that we might believe
in your presence even in our pain;
stretch our souls that we may go deeper
into the reality of your incarnation.

Part One: The Way

THE FIRST STATION: CONDEMNATION
Jesus is condemned to death

The sun was bright, almost blinding,
as he walked out of the clinic.
He had never seen the sun so bright, or so he thought.
He listened to the roar of the cars passing on the busy street
in front of him. He smelled the aroma of hot dogs
coming from a street vendor's cart nearby,
bought a bratwurst,
and walked the streets of downtown.
The brat was the best he had ever tasted.
He sat on a bench in the park and watched the people walk by.
Examining their faces, he wondered what stories were hidden
behind the wrinkles and lines etched around their eyes.
He heard the children playing in the sandbox
and climbing on the jungle gym.
A dog was reprimanded by its owner for barking at the children.
He leaned back on the bench and looked at the sky.
It had never been so clear as it was this afternoon.
He breathed deeply the cool, crisp March air
and coughed as he exhaled.
He was 29 years old and he had just been told
that he was HIV positive.
Now everything had changed.
He was dying.
In the face of death,
he decided it was a good time to start living.

■

Jesus is condemned to death.
He stands before Pilate and hears his death sentence.
How many today stand before the sentence of death:
the prisoner on death row;
the patient in the wing of the hospital for the terminally ill; the
young woman so depressed that she looks
at the bottle of pills on her dresser
and knows it is one way to end her pain.
Jesus stands with these people today.
He stands with the woman in Sarajevo who said
to a correspondent in January, 1994,
"How long are you going to sit there and watch us die?"
He stands with the poor ones who scramble for food
in the garbage dump of a fast-food restaurant
hoping for a few fries or a half-eaten hamburger
to calm the groan and ease the pain in their stomachs.
He stands behind the elderly woman sitting alone in her room
at the nursing home who forgets her past
and doesn't recognize her children and grandchildren
when they come to visit.
He stands with the parents at the grave of their only son
killed in a drive-by shooting that police say
was just another case of random violence.
He stands behind that young man sitting in the park
and looking up at the sky
as he sees the dreams for his future fly
in the wind of his doctor's words
who just told him he has AIDS.

■

The question this station along the way of the cross
raises for us is this:
Where do we stand?
As a Haitian proverb says,
"We see from where we stand."
So, what do we see from where we stand?
Too often we answer that question with ideology or labels.
We say we are
liberal or conservative;
progressive or traditional.
We identify ourselves with political causes or social concerns.
When it comes to issues in the Church today,
we are asked where we stand
on inclusive language or women priests.
There are a wide variety of problems and points of view
that call forth from us a response to the question,
where do we stand?
But now we are asked to answer that question
not from the head but from the heart.
Not from the mind but from the gut.
Not from the vantage point above the fray
but from down here below.

■

As we begin this sorrowful sojourn,
it is important to check our feet
because they tell us volumes about our faith.
Our first inclination is to find some comfortable shoes
for this walk of the cross;
shoes that won't pinch our feet
or cause us to rub blisters as we walk along the way.
But then we remember what God said to Moses

when God called him to be a prophet:
"Remove the sandals from your feet,
for the place where you stand is holy ground." [Ex. 3:5]
The place where we stand is holy ground.
The blood of the poor,
the accused,
the condemned
has seeped into the soil beneath our feet.
This is holy ground.
Our feet will feel the sharp pain
from pieces of broken dreams
hidden in the sand on the ground where we stand.
This is holy ground.
Our feet will kick up the dirt of our past mistakes
and hasty condemnations of others.
And God's mercy will make this holy ground.
We stand in the same place Jesus stands:
the place of condemnation, accusation, and rejection.
It is a place,
a starting point,
that will lead to a lonely hill outside the city of Jerusalem where
tears are shed
and hopes are shredded.
This is the place where we will find the meaning of redemption.
Where do we stand?

PRAYER

O God,
my feet have grown accustomed
to the feel of comfortable carpet.
Now you ask me to stand
on the cold concrete of those condemned.

You take my hand
and cause me to stand
on the muddy trails of the oppressed
where blood seeps between my toes.
You ask me to stand in dangerous alleys
where the homeless sleep
with bits of broken glass
etched upon their feet.
Help me to stand here, O God,
knowing that I stand with you.

THE SECOND STATION: CROSS
Jesus takes up his cross

On the wall of the room in the rectory
there was a picture depicting the Sacred Heart of Jesus.
I've seen this picture hundreds of times before
but acknowledge that I never paid much attention to it.
Looking closely, I noticed that the exposed heart of Jesus
looked like a bruised apple.
It was encircled by a crown of thorns.
A gash was etched on its right side
with blood streaming from the wound.
From the heart on all sides were rays of light.
The heart, though wounded, was still alive.
The heart, though bleeding, was still beating.

∎

Jesus had a bleeding heart.
He was liberal with his love.
That is why he accepted this cross thrust upon his shoulders.
He could have called down the elite armed forces of angels
who, like Stealth Bombers,
could fly so low as to be undetected by radar.
Pilate's paratroopers would not have stood a chance.
But he accepted the unjust decision of the court;
and then, rather than exhausting his appeals to a higher court,
he waived his right to sit on death row and accepted the cross.
He did it because his heart was already bleeding for

the suffering ones he had seen;
the sinful ones who were out of his reach;
the broken ones he had tried to mend;
the righteous ones he tried to teach.
This was the only way to bring order to a world in chaos.
Like his Divine Parent
who created light out of darkness,
a holy order out of chaos,
Jesus recognized that accepting the cross
would be his most creative act.
This was the only way to bring sanity to a world gone mad with
pride and prejudice,
violence and vindictiveness.
The way of the cross was the only reasonable response
to the irrational way in which people treated one another.
He had to enter the suffering; he had to enter the pain.
He could not stand idly by and hope that God would send
a rescue team to save him from this suffering.
He knew he was the rescue team.
He knew this was the way.

When our hearts are broken and woven back together
with thorns instead of thread,
we wonder if we wouldn't be better off dead.
When the anguish of betrayal causes our hearts to harden,
we pray to even the score.
When our loved ones leave us and we wonder why,
our hearts bleed.
Jesus accepted the cross because in his Sacred Heart
he knew our pain. And somehow, some way,
he wanted us to know that he understood.

Because he also stood under the weight of the wood of the
cross.
Though it nearly crushed him, he continued to stand.
Though his legs would grow wobbly and weak,
he would carry this cross because he knew
deep in his Sacred Heart
that there would be crosses in our lives
when we would say to God,
"This is too heavy! Take this one away!"
What crosses do we stand under today?
What are those sorrows that leave a gash on our heart?
We stop here long enough to ask the questions,
to feel the pain,
to know the sorrow,
to believe the gain.
The gain that comes when we know our pain
well enough to stand with others in theirs.
And when we do,
when we recognize the chaos within us and around us
as an opportunity for a creative response,
that crush we feel
is a thing called
love.

PRAYER

Of all the crosses on display in the chamber of sorrows,
I much prefer a different one.
Do you have a lighter model, God?
One not so burdensome;
one with a smoother finish, perhaps?
Okay, I'll take this one.
No pain, no gain.

But I must ask you, God,
even as this one crushes me,
isn't there some other way to love?

THE THIRD STATION: COLLAPSE
Jesus falls the first time

In Berkeley, California there is a street
called Telegraph Avenue. It is a stream
of commercial activity flowing from the campus
of the university there. An endless succession of shops,
some eclectic, many expensive,
beckon student and sightseer to stop and browse and buy.
All of society is represented on this avenue of adventure,
from the remnant to the wealthy.
From Saks Fifth Avenue to street merchants.
From 90's yuppies to 60's yippies.
From the preppies of today
to the poor of yesterday, today, and tomorrow.
One afternoon I took a stroll down Telegraph Avenue.
It began to rain so I sought refuge in a bookstore
with an enclosed sidewalk cafe. I figured a cup of coffee
and an Annie Dillard book would be more than enough
to keep me warm and out of the rain.
Just outside the glass windows of the coffee shop,
homeless men, women, and children huddled under the canopy,
trying to stay dry.
A basket, the kind you find in a church on Sunday morning,
was set in front of them.
Loose change formed a mosaic on the bottom of the basket.
No dollar bills. Paper currency would just get soggy in the rain.
A bus stopped on the street.
The sign on the bus said: "Homelessness happens."

I know. I saw it. It was happening right there in the rain
while I was inside, warm and dry.
A man looked at me through the glass.
The lines on his face were deep and timeless.
A map to the land of pain.
His eyes, though, were an oasis in the desert of his face.
Like a pool of deep, clear, blue water,
still and silent but not stagnant.
Not yet.
I wondered from what source fresh streams would come
to replenish his tears?
Somewhere, hidden in the deep blue of this one's ancient eyes,
there was a dream long since deferred.
I tried to drink from his well of experience
but he would not allow me to trespass.
When our eyes met, he looked down at the basket.
So I returned to my book.
This man, looking at me through that window,
reminded me of my own poverty. A poverty not of monetary
means but of spiritual resources.
He reminded me how poor I really am that I do not possess
the spiritual passion,
the practical means,
nor the political will
to free this one person from his prison of pain.
When the rain turned to drizzle,
I ventured out on the street again.
I looked at him and his family, dropped in some change,
and continued down the street.

■

That homeless family I saw on Telegraph Avenue depended
upon the "kindness of strangers" to stay alive.
This station suggests that we are all needy.
Even Jesus.
It doesn't take long for Jesus to collapse
under the weight of the wood.
When he falls this first time,
can we imagine his head hitting the cobblestone pavement
and splitting open?
Can we see the thorns push down and become embedded
in the crown of his head?
Do we notice the welts beginning to rise on the body of Christ?
Can we see those abrasions, those open cuts,
those long red wounds oozing blood on his back?
Can we see the bruises on the body of Christ?
If we can't, then may I suggest we turn back
because the rest of the journey will not
make much difference to us.
We will be like spectators at a traffic accident,
looking for gore and missing the meaning.
But if we see these bruises and abrasions on the body of Christ,
really see them,
then we will dare to make a difference.
We will do what we can to stop the bleeding.
For only when the bleeding is stopped,
can the healing process begin.

■

When we fall under the weight of our crosses and losses in life,
the temptation is to stay low,
stay on the ground,
and hope that someone comes along to give us a hand, a heart.

But when someone else falls,
the temptation is,
"Don't get involved. It's none of my business."
So at this station along the way of suffering,
we might acknowledge this:
that we have all fallen down every now and then.
When we take the time to notice that we are all on our knees,
we might see some of those broken pieces of our lives
scattered on the ground.
And how brightly they shine in the light of another's eyes.

PRAYER

I recall, O God,
the story of one of your saints, Dorothy Day,
who one day came upon a women whose face
had been disfigured by cancer.
This woman reached out her hand to Dorothy, asking for help.
St. Dorothy held the woman in her arms
and kissed her cancerous face.
Her lips touched the gaping hole
where the woman's nose once had been.
In explaining why she did it, she said something like this:
"We can do anything when we learn a little bit more about
love."
Help me, Divine Lover,
to learn a little bit more about this kind of love.
Though I stumble and fall,
help me to see that I'm in good company.
The company of those you love the most:
the fallen, the forsaken, the forgotten.
When I learn a little more about this love,
even though a lump may form in my throat,

and I will wonder from what source this courage swells,
I will put my lips upon another's face,
and know I kiss the face of God.

THE FOURTH STATION: AFFECTION
Jesus meets his mother

A Muslim folktale tells the story
of an old woman who had a camel.
It was her only source of income. But then it was stolen.
There was a rich man who had thirty camels.
Among them this woman saw her camel. Everyone was amazed.
Why would this rich man steal this poor woman's only camel?
And how in the world could she know for sure that this camel
she thought she recognized was really hers?
But she insisted it was. So they told her to prove it.
"I can prove it," the old woman said.
"Kill the camel and open her chest.
On her heart you will find a scar."
The camel was killed and sure enough on her heart
they found a scar. Everyone was astonished.
The rich man gave the old woman two camels
but as he gave them to her he asked,
"How could you know there would be a scar on her heart?"
"It is simple," the old woman said.
"Two years ago the son of this camel was killed by a wolf.
The camel was so sad that I knew
it must have left a mark on her heart."

■

There is a scar on Mary's heart
as she stands amid the clamorous crowd

hurling insults and accusations at her beloved son.
Her eyes can scarcely see his bruised and battered body
through her tears.
But can we imagine their eyes meeting,
if just for a moment,
and the deep affection held in that sacred stare?
Long ago Mary had been warned about this anguish.
Recall when Mary and Joseph brought the child to the temple;
the old prophet, Simeon, looked into Mary's eyes and said,
This child is destined to be the downfall and the rise
of many in Israel, a sign that will be opposed
and you yourself shall be pierced with a sword—
so that the thoughts of many hearts may be laid bare.
[Luke 2:34-35]
She knows now what the old man meant.
The opposition to her son is loud and clear.
She hears the jeers and remembers it wasn't so long ago
that her son rode into town to cheers and songs of praise.
But now the adulation had turned to accusation.
The old man had told Mary her heart would be pierced.
As she watches her son struggle under the weight of the cross,
she knows this scar will survive.

■

What thoughts of ours are laid bare by Mary's pierced heart?
What are we thinking, feeling, as we look at Mary and Jesus
making eye contact along the way?
Mary's scarred heart solicits from us a desire
to trace the scars engraved on our own hearts.
Recently a woman, a mother—I'll call her Janice—told me
of one of her scars.
In the winter of 1992,

Janice and her husband Phil were expecting their fourth child.
Because they had three other children,
Janice was working full-time outside the home
to make ends meet.
But she couldn't take the stress of both the work and pregnancy
so she took sick leave from her job.
Seven months into the pregnancy,
Janice went in for an ultra-sound.
The doctor told her there were serious problems with the baby.
There was a tumor on the brain.
There were heart problems and physical deformities.
The baby had a genetic defect and the doctor
told Janice and Phil that babies born with these genetic defects
could live up to a year with the help of machines.
Janice and Phil debated what to do.
They listened to family and friends.
They cried and prayed.
And they also planned.
"Pre-planning a funeral for a baby," Janice said,
"That's not what we were supposed to be doing.
But we were not sure what to do.
Some suggested an out-of-state abortion.
I even considered what an easy way out that would be."
A month or so later, Janice gave birth to a girl.
She was given the name they had picked out for her months
before, Elizabeth.
She was baptized and lived for 35 minutes.
Janice and Phil's other three children came up to see Elizabeth
and to hold her and say goodbye.
During Elizabeth's funeral a storm knocked out
all the power at the funeral home.
Candles lit the family's way.

"So it is with our faith," Janice told me.
"Jesus is the light that guides us on the path.
And the light grows brighter with every step."

■

Janice had traced the scar left on her heart
by her daughter's death and found a measure of healing
in knowing that the one who walks this way of the cross
is the light of the world.
Perhaps that is what Mary was sensing in her soul that day
as the shadow of her suffering son crossed her path.
When their eyes met and they saw each other
through the blood, the sweat, the tears,
Mary recognized her son as the light,
the only light,
that could help her see her way on this path
of a pierced heart.

PRAYER

Mary, mother of Jesus,
stand shoulder to shoulder with us today.
Give us the courage not to look away
but to look toward the light.
Your son radiates redemption and illuminates hope.
The light in your son's eyes
glows in the darkness of these days to guide our path,
to show us the way.
As you held this light in your hands when he was young,
help us to hold in our hands and hearts
the hope of reconciliation
and the look of love.

THE FIFTH STATION: COURAGE
Simon of Cyrene helps Jesus carry the cross

On June 8, 1987, my older brother, Ed, committed suicide.
Ed had suffered the last ten years of his life
from a mental illness known as paranoid schizophrenia,
a terrible and terrifying disease that turned
Ed's life into a living hell.
During those years, Ed was in and out of mental hospitals.
On constant medication to still the voices he heard in his mind,
Ed lost his job, his friends, and ultimately his life.
I presided and preached at Ed's funeral.
It was the most difficult thing I have ever had to do as a priest
because this pain was so personal.
The thing about suicide is that you never have a chance
to say goodbye.
I wanted to say goodbye to Ed at his funeral;
and I wanted to name the anguish that Ed had experienced
the last years of his life.
I wanted people to know what my brother had been through;
what Ed had suffered;
and what he taught us through his suffering.
But I didn't know how I would get through that Mass.
Shortly before we were to begin the funeral,
Tren Meyers,
a good friend and a priest in my community,
who was there to share those days of grief with my family and
me, invited those of us who were concelebrating

to join hands in prayer.
I don't remember the words he said,
but I will never forget the experience.
It was a feeling of being lifted up.
Tren's prayer,
and the knowledge of all the prayers from those
who knew Ed, my family, and myself,
lifted me up and freed me to name the pain;
freed me to remember Ed.
Tren came out of the crowd and helped me and my family
carry a cross that was crushing us.

■

Why was Simon in town that day?
Had he come all the way from Cyrene to visit his family
and celebrate the Passover?
Or was he just coming in for some supplies to take with him
back to his farm?
Mark says he was "the father of Alexander and Rufus"
and "was coming in from the fields" when
"they pressed him into service to carry the cross." [Mark 15:21]
Did he just happen to be passing by when the soldiers pushed
him out of the crowd and into the street
to help Jesus carry the cross?
Was it a matter of being at the wrong place at the wrong time?
After all, he probably had another way to go.
Or was he at the right place at the right time?
Now he would follow the way of the cross
and his life would be changed forever.
One cannot help another carry a cross without being changed.
Now Simon of Cyrene's life was claimed by God.
This was his baptism by fire.

Though the soldiers who grabbed him and forced him to help
Jesus didn't know it at the time—
all they saw was a poor farmer trying to mind his own business—
they were buying Simon's soul for God.
For now Simon was a witness to the execution;
he was no longer a spectator but a participant
in the passion of Christ.
Whether he resisted or not is no longer the point.
His witness of coming out from the crowd
to help Jesus along the way is a memory
that lingers in our minds and lives on in our faith.

■

When we are part of a large crowd, we can remain anonymous.
Just another face among a thousand other faces.
But when we take the step—or are pushed—out from the crowd,
we stand in the spotlight of someone else's suffering.
Sharing in another's passion holds the promise of transformation.
Then we begin to see the cross, our own and other's,
as a ladder to the very heart of God.
I learned that lesson the day we buried my brother Ed.
Though the pain of his death was a cross too heavy to bear,
the prayer of my friend, Tren,
and the compassion of others reminded me again
that Christ was present in our suffering.
God knew what we were going through.
And now Simon of Cyrene did too.
When have we stepped out of a crowd of bystanders
and made a difference in another's story?
How were we changed by this single step, this initial attempt,
to help another carry the cross?

PRAYER

We stand by the way, O God.
We are guilty bystanders to the suffering we see
in our world today.
But we know we cannot stand here very long.
We must move.
We must claim our name for you have claimed our soul.
Give us a push or give us the courage to come out from the
crowd to bring some healing,
some small glimmer of hope,
to another so burdened by sorrow.

Part Two: The Truth

THE SIXTH STATION: COMPASSION
Veronica wipes the face of Jesus

Katherine is blind in one eye
and the other causes her great pain.
Her eyes are very dry and she has to take drops
to keep the eyes moist.
"I can't cry," she told me. "But I cry in here."
She pointed to her heart.
Katherine worked for a while as a nurse in Boston.
She worked with the incurably ill and remembered being present
with many at the moment of death.
It was obviously a powerful experience for Katherine
that was repeated many times.
She showed me around her small house.
I saw a picture of her daughter.
"She passed away many years ago," Katherine said quietly.
There was great pain etched in her dry eyes.
Though nearly blind, Katherine reads the Scripture each day.
I noted in her well-worn Bible with large print
that her bookmark was on Luke.
"I like the Gospels," she said.
"It is almost as if I'm right there with Jesus."
Katherine also has favorite stories from the Hebrew Testament—
Jacob wrestling with the angel,
Joseph and his coat of many colors,
Ruth, Esther, and others.
But Katherine's favorite religious figure
is not even mentioned in Scripture.

"When I make the Stations of the Cross in church," she told me,
"I spend the longest time in front of the sixth station.
There is something about Veronica wiping the face of Jesus
that moves me very much."
That's when she told me how she sat at her daughter's side
during those last few hours.
Her daughter was burning up with fever
and Katherine sat by her side with a cool towel
pressed against her daughter's forehead.
Katherine, like Veronica,
ministered to someone she loved who was dying.
The pictures of her daughter that crowd her room remind
Katherine of her daughter's beauty.
She remembers.
That is why she spends so long in front of this station.
She remembers.

■

Who is this Veronica?
There is no mention of her in any of the passion narratives.
In fact, her name is not mentioned anywhere in Scripture.
Where did she come from?
Why is she here?
It was a tradition of the Church in Jerusalem
that as Jesus struggled through the streets of the city,
carrying his cross,
a woman broke through the crowd to wipe
the blood, sweat, and tears
from the face of Jesus.
And when she looked at the veil,
there was an imprint of his face.
Whether this event actually took place is not our concern.

What is our focus is the compassion the story conveys.
Could it be that Veronica was wearing this veil
over her face in grief for what was taking place
and what was about to happen to Jesus?
Could it be that her mourning was her motivation
to run past the centurions who were in charge of crowd control?
Could it be it was a cool towel that she pressed
against the feverish face of Jesus?

■

Someone we love is about to die.
We do what we must to make our beloved more comfortable.
We prop up the pillows.
We stay close and wipe our beloved's forehead.
We don't worry about other things that must be done
or other promises that must be kept.
No, this one is our focus.
This dying one receives all of our compassion.
Every ounce of it.
And when our beloved dies, we are left
with photographs and memories.
But even more,
we are left with the imprint of that one's face upon our heart.

■

Who cries out for our compassion today?
Who longs for our tender touch?
Like Katherine, we spend time at this station
because we are moved by Veronica's extraordinary act
of kindness. Like Katherine,
we sense meaning in her action because we have been there too.

We have the photographs,
the memories,
the imprint to prove it.
We have seen the face of Jesus.
We have wiped his brow and tasted his tears.
We know.
This is where Veronica's compassion and ours is found:
in our own experiences of mourning the death
of someone we love.
When motivated by such empathy,
barriers melt away under the heat of our concern.
We will do anything to be near the one we love
at the moment of death.
If it means breaking through a police barricade,
we will do it.
If it means breaking hospital rules for visitation,
we will do it.
If it means flying across the country on a moment's notice,
we will do it.
We will do anything for love of the one who is about to die.
Like Veronica with Jesus;
like Katherine with her daughter,
we are absorbed by the presence of the one we love.
Like a human sponge, we soak in all the memories
and love we have shared with our beloved through the years;
and all the pain and suffering and distance as well.
We soak it all in and find in being absorbed
by the other's presence, we can serve her
in a way we never imagined before.
Our ability to serve others with compassion and care
is found first in our willingness to be healed;
in our desire to be touched

and made whole by the presence of God in our lives.
Perhaps by leaving his face on Veronica's veil,
Jesus reminds us that just as we will do anything
for love of those who are dying,
we might also do anything for love of those who are living.
To see his face imprinted on the faces of each and every one.

PRAYER

God of Love,
the face of your Son was absorbed into the veil of Veronica,
a courageous woman of compassion.
Instill within us the spirit of this saintly woman.
Help us to absorb your divine presence
in the faces of each other.
With indelible ink,
imprint your image once again upon our lives.

THE SEVENTH STATION: AGONY
Jesus falls a second time

I remember a friend saying to me when I was going through
a particularly difficult time in my life,
"There's something beautiful up ahead."
I wanted to believe her
but when all one tastes is the dirt from the dusty trail
after a fall,
it was hard to see the beauty.

■

Is this the view Jesus sees from ground level
as he falls a second time:
"There's something beautiful up ahead"?
He has lost so much blood he can barely move.
Each step is filled with excruciating agony.
But he stays on the ground for only a short time
to catch his breath;
to steal a moment's rest.
He knows this pain will pass
because he knows the beauty that beckons him;
the loveliness of life that awaits him;
the radiance of resurrection that will reflect forever
and for all time.
Though his body is so weary from the scourging
and the weight of the heavy cross,
he knows this pain will pass.

■

But while the pain is present,
I grow as impatient as a child
climbing in the car for a family trip
and saying as the car pulls out of the driveway,
"How long before we get there?"
That is our prayer at this station:
"How long, O Lord?"
When we started this journey, that was the temptation:
to get it over with as quickly as possible
because we don't like to fall.
We want to rush past the pain and get to the glory
as quickly as possible.
But we know life doesn't work that way.
Certainly Jesus didn't live that way.
Instead he went the way that included a fall or two or three.

■

If we are afraid of falling, we will never walk again.
If our focus is on not falling,
we will miss the thrill of living.
Remember the great circus act, "The Flying Walendas"?
It was a family of performers who glided through the air
with the "greatest of ease."
They dared the forces of gravity by walking on wires
stretched high across canyons and chasms of every sort.
In 1978, Karl Walenda, the founder of the troupe,
died when he fell trying to walk a wire
between two ten-story buildings in San Juan, Puerto Rico.
In a magazine article about his tragic death,
Walenda's wife was quoted as saying:

"All Karl thought about for three months prior to his death
was falling. It was the first time he had ever thought
about that, and it seemed to me
that he put all his energies into NOT falling
rather than WALKING that tightrope."
On this way of the cross,
we walk a tightrope between terror and tenderness;
tragedy and triumph.
On this way of love, we walk without nets.
We wonder who will catch us when we fall.
But that is not the question.
The question is:
Where do we put our energies,
on our fear of falling or our faith in walking?
In the walk of life,
we will stumble every now and then over our own fears
and fall flat on our faces.
We will trip over our tendency
to think of ourselves first
as we put the needs of others somewhere down the road.
We will slip on peels of pride
and stagger under the weight of loss.
From all these falls,
our egos will get bruised,
our faith will get tested,
our love will get proven,
and our heart will get examined.
What's that old saying:
falling is the easy part, it's getting up again that's difficult? We
can get up after a fall
when we know the beauty will remain.
When we fall in love and the relationship ends,

we can get up and love again.
When we fall in grief as a loved one dies,
we can get up and live again.
When we fall in sin and the guilt keeps us down,
we can get up and be forgiven again.
Jesus fell in love for us.
For whom will we fall?

PRAYER

O God,
after a fall
you know how hard it is for us to get back up again.
We would prefer to stay on the ground and let the sound
of the laughing crowd to grow distant
before we pick ourselves up,
dust ourselves off,
and continue on the way.
How long, O God, will you let us fall?
How long, O Lord, before we get to where we want to go?
How much more dirt do we have to taste
before we can sip the sweet wine of your compassion?
With faces pressed against the trail of tears,
we hear you whisper the words
that give us the courage to get up again.
"Whenever you fall for one of these least brothers and sisters,
you fall for me."
After such a fall,
we know that the pain will pass
but the beauty will remain.

THE EIGHTH STATION: FIDELITY

Jesus meets the women of Jerusalem

My vote for "Best Supporting Disciple" in the Gospels
is the mother of James and John.
We don't know her name but she is mentioned in three key
scenes. In the first, she doesn't even appear on screen.
Can we imagine this woman saying to her husband,
"Zeb, where are the boys? I made their favorite fish"?
Zebedee tells her that James and John won't be home for
supper because that afternoon they dropped their nets in the
boat, left him low and dry,
and walked off with an itinerant preacher named Jesus.
"The boys have run off to join this guy's
traveling salvation show,"
Zebedee tells her.
This news must have been quite upsetting to our supporting
disciple because she left the fish to fry
and went off in search of her boys.
She followed their trail
until that day she caught up with them and said to Jesus:
"I want you to promise me that my boys will sit,
one at your right and one at your left,
when you enter your reign."
In this scene she is cast as the ambitious mother
who is trying to get her sons high places in the company.
This comes no doubt from her own passion and love
for wanting only the very best for them.

Of course, it could be that the boys put her up to it.
"Go ahead, ma, ask him, ask him."
So, this woman who used to tell her sons to drink their milk
now hears that they must drink from a cup filled
with suffering and sorrow.
This mother who told her boys to take a bath before supper
now hears they will swim in a bath of pain.
We never learn her name
and yet she probably understood even better than her boys
what Jesus meant when he said he was "going up to Jerusalem,"
because she shows up one more time in this passion play:
on a lonely hill outside of Jerusalem.
Among those huddled at the foot of the cross are
Mary Magdalene, Mary, the mother of James and Joseph,
and the mother of Zebedee's sons.
She is one of those weeping women we remember
in the way of the cross when Jesus stops and says,
"Daughters of Jerusalem, do not weep for me.
Weep for yourselves and for your children." [Luke 23:28]

■

How many tears this woman must have shed for her boys,
James and John.
How many tears are being shed today
by mothers for their children;
by sisters for their brothers;
by daughters for their fathers.
The tears of women around the world water the earth this day.
I think of the Guatemalan women I met when I visited there.
Each morning, they gathered at the well
to wash their clothes and share their stories.
Some of these women have had husbands and children

kidnaped and killed by the guerrilla forces.
These were the mothers of the disappeared.
Their tears were real—
and so was their faith.
I remember how the clouds hung low over Lake Atitlan
the day we visited there.
The volcanoes were masked in mystery.
These were holy mountains,
made sacred by Mother Earth's angry eruptions.
I wondered if our mother is upset at the injustice
that binds her poor. She shakes her green clad body to display
her displeasure at what her people suffer.
Guatemala is a land of contradictions.
From the luxury hotel on one side of Lake Atitlan
to the garbage that litters the land
on the other side of the lake.
When we had finished our tour of Santiago de Atitlan,
as we were about to embark to the other side of the lake,
an old woman invited me to take her picture for one quesella.
I could not resist. It was a bargain.
This woman, her face wrapped in wrinkles;
her body clothed in native garb,
showed me wisdom.
The wisdom of the land.
The gentleness of a grandmother.
The warmth of a forgotten love.
I do not know how many years marked the lines on her face.
I only know that this woman knew the truth.
I could see it in her toothless grin.
I could sense it in her insistent yet gentle gaze.
I could see it in the dignity with which she posed
for the picture.

I have this woman's face looking at me now
from the wall in my room.
Whenever I look at those eyes, those wrinkles, that dignity,
just for a moment I think I know what wisdom is.

■

Real authority in life comes from being attuned
to the sighs and cries of others.
Real authority comes when one seeks to understand
what one cannot possibly comprehend—
like this woman, a mother, who is told by Jesus
that he must go to Jerusalem to be flogged and crucified.
She heard this and believed it
or else she wouldn't have been one of those few
who were there at the end.
Though her boys had the privilege of going with him
into the Garden of Gethsemane, they fell asleep
and then ran away when the heat in the garden got too hot.
This woman, the mother of Zebedee's boys, stayed awake.
This woman, accustomed to a supporting role
and most comfortable away from the spotlight,
was there at the end.
She was able to drink from the same cup,
bathe in the same pain, as Jesus.
Unlike her sons, she would not desert him.
She was faithful to the end.
So the winner as best supporting disciple is this woman—
one who knew much about losing one's name
so as to be identified with another name: Christ.
One who knew about losing herself in her love for others.

PRAYER

"Don't cry for me," Jesus says.
Weep for one another.
Weep for the poor ones,
the abandoned ones,
the disappeared, the depressed, the oppressed.
Weep for those in our world that cry out for justice.
Let your tears become streams of mercy and compassion.
Let others drink from the pool
of your passionate presence for peace.
God of Mercy,
give us the gift of tears.

THE NINTH STATION: COMMITMENT
Jesus falls the third time

At one time in her life,
Charlene was filled with promise, happiness, success.
Then one day she was diagnosed with multiple sclerosis.
Charlene fell for the first time.
Eight months later, her husband of six years
left her because he could not handle the idea
that he might have to care
for Charlene if her condition worsened.
She was alone, 1,500 miles from her family.
Charlene fell a second time.
She had not been particularly close to God
but the morning after her husband left her,
she decided to pray.
For reasons she cannot describe,
she decided she would not give in to the diagnosis of her illness
nor the death of her relationship with her husband.
She would continue to fight.
She would get up again.
Later that same year,
a person wielding a knife slashed her hand.
She put her hand to her throat just in time
but was cut across the entire width of her palm.
The cut was deep enough to sever tendons.
It took stitches and time to heal the wound.
Charlene had fallen a third time.
During this time of her physical recovery,

her life began to change.
Charlene began serious discernment about another way of life.
She returned home.
Through conversations with her mentor and persistent prayer,
Charlene discovered a call to religious life.
She kept this private until the time when it was clear
to her that her motives were valid and she was not looking
for a way to escape the pain of her past.
Charlene found a way to say yes to a new life.
It was the way of the cross.
She knew she was not alone.
Now she shares her story;
she isn't shy about telling others of the Great Spy
in the sky who keeps an eye
out for her.
Wrestling with her grief, anger, and illness;
pinned to the canvas for what she thought
was the best of two out of three falls,
Charlene walks her talk
and has found her destiny.

■

Our journey on this way of the cross
is measured not in steps but in falls—three falls.
Jesus falls the third time.
Three strikes and you're out.
But not Jesus.
He gets up again to continue the journey
toward the place of the skull.
He realizes that his life,
lived intensely,
means more than how many times you fall

or even how many people you touch.
It means that you make a difference in the lives
of those you encounter along the way.
It means that no matter how often you fall,
courage is found in the getting up again.
It means that though the road may seem long and arduous,
strewn with rocks and littered with broken promises
that cause one to trip and stumble and fall flat on one's face,
there is a destination here.
There is a destiny here.
There is a life here—a life fully lived.

PRAYER

Help us to see, O Gracious God,
that our lives our temporary;
that our death is certain.
But in the span of our years,
may we touch others with the beauty of life.
May our lives be like brushes
that paint on the scarred canvas of our world
a landscape of vibrant colors.
Though the brush may fall from our hands now and then,
may our hope never fail.
May we live the destiny that is ours:
the life that is you.

THE TENTH STATION: DOUBT AND SHAME
Jesus is stripped of his clothes

A friend of mine once told me when I was struggling in
the seminary about whether to stay or leave
that he never entertained doubts about his vocation.
Once he entered the community, once he was ordained,
he never looked back.
Entertaining doubt.
Now there's an interesting phrase.
How often I have invited Doubt over for dinner.
How often I have fixed Doubt a drink as we sat by the window
or the fire and wondered out loud about life, community,
priesthood, love, vocation, and other matters of the soul.
Yes, I have entertained the whole Doubt family on occasion:
big doubts, small ones, old ones that never die,
and young ones born in ministry and living in community.
Faith becomes jealous when I have Doubt over for dinner.
I've known of their feud for a long time and every now and then
I would mention it to Faith. I would say,
"I believe Doubt can be a friend
that will deepen my love for you, my Faith."
Especially when I go on the road and preach,
some Doubts come along for the ride.
Though I hope my Faith is carried in every word,
Doubt still lingers in the margins looking for an ellipsis,
a pause, an opportunity to jump in and fill the void.
I was surprised when my friend told me he never doubted his
call. Most of us do from time to time.

But this man was one who, when he put his hand to the plow,
never looked back.
He knew it was God guiding the plow, turning up the dirt,
making straight furrows in the fields.
As for me, I keep looking over my shoulder.
Though I keep plowing—my Faith tells me to keep going—
Doubt often whispers,
"Better check that furrow you just plowed."

■

If ever there was a station on this holy way that would cause
Doubt to make an appearance on the scene, this one is it.
Stripped of his clothing,
standing naked before his accusers,
did Jesus look over his shoulder and wonder why
he had not listened more attentively to the Doubt
that crowded his mind in the Garden of Gethsemane
the night before?
That moment when he prayed,
"Father, let this cup pass me by"?
But his Faith got the better of Doubt in that struggle
as he added, "But your will, not mine, be done."

■

Now Doubt's evil cousin, Shame, enters the picture.
We talk of entertaining Doubt but never about entertaining
Shame. Shame has a twin sister called Guilt.
We invite Guilt over often and encourage her to stay
for an extended visit.
But not Shame.
We want to avoid her at every turn.

We never want to invite Shame over for supper.
We want to leave Shame out on the porch and welcome instead
one of our favorite members of this family of feelings, Fame.
Stripped of everything we own,
from clothes to consolation,
we stand naked at this station.
We feel exhausted and exposed;
vulnerable and victimized.
This nakedness is not born from innocence or desire.
It is the result of shame.
We want to scream, "I will not be put to shame!"
But we have no choice.
Others put us in this place where we'd rather not be.

■

Her mother was killed in the bombing of Berlin.
In 1951, Anna came to the United States.
She knew very little English and the few words she did know
were spoken with a very thick German accent.
Shortly after her arrival, she went to church to go
to confession. As she knelt to confess her sins,
she struggled with the words.
The priest on the other side of the screen grew impatient.
He began to criticize her, saying she only came to this country
in pursuit of the all-mighty American dollar.
He scolded her and condemned her for being German.
When Anna walked out of the confessional that day,
she felt so ashamed, so small, so shaken.
And when she walked out of church that day,
she never went back.
For forty years, she stayed away from the table.
The wound inflicted by that priest's words continued to deepen.

Every now and then, the wound festered.
In the middle 1960s, a friend of Anna's brought her brother,
a priest, to see her. They visited for a while and Anna told her
story to the priest. Anger was etched in her words.
So much anger that this priest told her,
"You are not ready to come back."
Many more years passed and Anna stayed away from church.
Then, in 1991, this priest stopped to see Anna.
She told her story again,
this time with tears.
As she wept over the loss of her church, if not her faith,
the priest said to her, "Anna, you are ready to return."
The next Sunday, Anna was back at the table
for the first time in forty years.
She has not missed a day since.

■

If truth be told,
we would prefer to feel like those priests the prophet Jeremiah
referred to in Chapter 8 of his book. You know, the ones who
say, "Peace, peace! though there is no peace."
Jeremiah says of them,
"they know not how to blush." [vv. 11,12]
Instead, we hear the shouts, "Shame on you!"
We take it all inside and so come to know
what Jeremiah felt when he cried:
My grief is incurable,
my heart within me is faint...
Is there no balm in Gilead,
no physician there?
Why grows not new flesh

over the wound of the daughter of my people?
[Jeremiah 8:18,22]
This wound of shame is so deep
that there is no balm in Gilead or on Golgotha to heal it.
And so, a prayer stored deep in our soul comes to the surface:
In you our fathers and mothers trusted;
they trusted, and you delivered them.
To you they cried, and they escaped;
in you they trusted, and they were not put to shame.
[Psalm 22:5-6]
This may be the only prayer we can say
when our nakedness is covered with shame.
It is a prayer that comes from a soul that knows shame.
It is a prayer that rises from our own experience
of doubting that anything good might come out of this;
and from our own experience of being "put to shame."
With this prayer stirring within our souls,
we plow ahead.
We don't look back.
We focus our eyes straight ahead and trust that God
will somehow, some way, deliver us.
Though this humiliation
may tempt us to want to crawl into a hole and hide,
we know the soul has already dug the hole
that will lead to our great escape.

■

PRAYER

Open my ears, O God of Grace,
that I may hear the rousing word your prophet speaks.
With his well-trained tongue,

he stirs my weary bones with these words of hope:
"I gave my back to those who beat me,
my cheeks to those who plucked my beard;
my face I did not shield from buffets and spitting.
The Lord God is my help, therefore I am not disgraced;
I have set my face like flint,
knowing that I shall not be put to shame."
[Isaiah 50:6-7]

Part Three: The Life

THE ELEVENTH STATION: NAILED
Jesus is nailed to the cross

Seventeen years ago, her daughter was murdered.
Her daughter's brother-in-law was convicted of the crime.
He spent a few years in prison.
She told me she remains close to her daughter's husband
and his mom and dad—the murderer's brother and parents—
and is trying to forgive.
"As long as I keep trying," she said.

■

She's right, of course.
The important thing is not that we are able to forgive
as Jesus forgave.
The important thing is that we keep on trying.
Another woman has been visiting a young friend
in the hospital who is terminally ill.
This young friend's husband left her when she got sick.
Now she is curled up in a fetal position,
depressed, and wanting only to die.
This woman who visits her told me,
"I wanted so much to fix this situation.
To ease this friend's pain.
She lets me touch her but I don't know if I can reach her.
Now I know that there are some things, some pain,
I just can't fix.
The most I can do is sit with her and help her cry."

■

The sound of the pounding of the nails echoes in our souls now.
We can try to cover our ears so we don't have to hear
the anguished cry of the one whose hands and feet
are punctured by spikes the size of swords,
or so it seems.
I prick my finger with a pin, I bleed.
I slice my skin with a carving knife, I scream.
I suck the blood from a paper cut and curse.
None of these come close to what we now experience
on this hill of horrors.
Not even close.
But maybe that woman whose daughter was murdered
knows something about the feeling of being nailed to a cross.
Maybe that young woman who prays to die and the friend who
stays by her side know the feeling of being crucified.
Maybe we do too.
But if we do, it's not easy to remember being crucified.
It's not pleasant bringing to mind those experiences
when we've been nailed to a cross or nailed by a loss.
But the sound of the hammers pounding on flesh and wood
provide us with instant recall.
The scabs from these wounds are ripped away.
The stitches are pulled out with violent force.
Our incurable wounds are allowed to breathe again.
And the pain is almost too much to bear.

■

A woman with tears streaming down her face,
came up to me after a talk I gave on the losses and crosses
we carry with us and said to me,

"My son died of AIDS four years ago."
Name the pain.
Oftentimes, that is all we can do.
Name it.
We can't cure it or get rid of it.
We can only name it and claim it as our own.
That is why the veneration of the cross on Good Friday
is such a powerful ritual.
When there is no other place to put the pain we name and
claim, we can put it here at the foot of the cross.
When we kneel before the cross of Christ stained
with his precious blood, we know we are not alone.
When we kiss the wood of the cross,
we become intimate with our own wounds.
When we listen to the wood, we hear the voice of God saying,
"I love you. I share your pain."
The most difficult experience in life is not that we have pain or
experience suffering or know the meaning of sorrow;
the most difficult experience in life is having to carry
the pain, the suffering, the sorrow
alone.
The cross shouts this:
"You do not have to bear this pain alone!"
The blood of the cross screams this:
"I am with you, drawing you close to my own broken heart."

█

Now that his flesh is fastened to the wood,
the soldiers lift the cross and plant it firmly in the ground. From a
distance, this action rekindles a memory.
"Just as Moses lifted up the serpent in the desert,

*so the Son of Man must be lifted up that all who believe
may have eternal life." [John 3:14]*
In this action of being raised up on the cross,
Jesus draws to himself all the pain,
all the suffering,
all the sin of the world to his very self.
Just as Moses lifted up the bronze serpent in the desert
to save the people from the plague of snakes,
using the very symbol of the evil they were experiencing
to free them from the evil,
so Jesus is nailed to the cross.
Crucifixion was cruel and unusual punishment,
reserved for the most heinous of crimes.
The cross,
symbol of brutality, execution, and evil,
becomes the symbol of our freedom.
When Jesus is lifted up on the cross,
he draws the poison of sin and death from our lives.
The cross,
symbol of death,
becomes our symbol of life.
The cross we are nailed to now names our pain.
The cross we are nailed to now claims our victory.
The cross we are nailed to now lifts us up and sets us free.
We stand here in disbelief.
How is this possible? How can this be?
But if we've been to the cross, we know.
If we keep trying to forgive, we know.
If we stop trying to fix another's pain, we understand.
If we keep our eyes focused on this cross,
and our ears attuned to the sound of the pounding
of the nails,

we will begin to hear the overture to a new anthem for all ages.
For when he is lifted up,
the first strains of the song of salvation are heard
across the skies
so "that all who believe may have eternal life in him."
[John 3:15]

PRAYER

We stand now, O Healing Spirit,
beneath the symbol that the medical profession uses
to demonstrate their desire to heal:
a snake coiled around a pole.
It is like the one Moses used in the desert to save his people.
But this is not the symbol we place on the wall of our bedroom
to guard us when we sleep;
or in our churches to remind us to stay awake.
The symbol we use in the sacred spaces of our lives is a cross.
The crucifix calls us to believe that healing is possible
even when there is no cure.
This symbol seems more real
because with all the modern medical miracles
which enable people to live longer,
doctors are still confronted with the reality
that every one of their patients will die.
Though doctors and nurses pledge that they will do
whatever is within their power to preserve human life
because death is their enemy,
there will come a day when they must be resigned
to the fact that death has won again.
"There's nothing more we can do," they will say.
But you, O God, are our Divine Physician.
You bring us healing even when there is no hope.

As your Son is lifted up on this cross,
lift from us our fears.
Lift us up in your love, O Lord,
and help us to believe.

THE TWELFTH STATION: DEATH
Jesus dies on the cross

Remember that young man I mentioned at our first station?
The young man who was told by his doctor
that he was HIV-positive?
Well, I met his parents on a retreat I was giving.
During the week, I noticed this man, I'll call him Al,
wearing a button with the U.S. postage stamp
of the red ribbon symbolizing concern and awareness for people
living with AIDS. I thanked him for wearing it.
That's when he told me his son, Adam, died of AIDS in 1989.
"He was gay," Al said to me.
"He told us he was gay when he was 19.
I told him it didn't make any difference to me.
You're my son. I love you."
Adam, Al's son, died at the age of 33.
Sharon came over and told me the rest of the story.
"You know when I was growing up and heard people say
that they prayed for a happy death,
I never knew what that meant. I do now.
Adam died a happy, peaceful death.
After his diagnosis, he spent the last years of his life
going public about having AIDS.
He would speak to groups and appear on local talks shows
in the city where he lived to raise people's awareness.
He even appeared on the cover of the city magazine
to tell his story."
I could see in Al's and Sharon's eyes they were proud of their

son. They were proud that he raised awareness
and heightened compassion. And they were grateful
that when their son died, he died a happy death
with his parents and his lover at his side—
the people, Sharon told me, Adam said he wanted to be there
for him when he died.
"He accomplished everything he set out to do in his life,"
Al said. "He did it all in a shorter time than most do."
Sharon and Al are faithful folks who stood by their son
because of their love for him.
They were not ashamed that he was gay.
They were not ashamed that he died of AIDS.
Though they feel deeply his loss in their life,
his death from AIDS is not some terrible little secret they feel
they have to keep to themselves.

■

As we stop at this station, our souls are thirsty.
We hear Jesus say, "I am thirsty." [John 19:28]
As John tells the story,
the soldiers soak a sponge with "common wine"
and raise it to the lips of Jesus.
Then he said, "Now it is finished." [John 19:30]
With the bitter taste of this common wine lingering on his lips,
Jesus dies.
Our souls thirst for the uncommon wine of compassion.
We long to sip and bring to our lips
the best bottle from the wine cellar of our souls:
the sweet wine of our liberation.
This uncommon vintage gives our lives meaning.
And isn't that what our souls are thirsty for?
Ultimately, we do not thirst for fame or fortune,

comfort and security,
but for meaning.
We want our lives to matter.
We want our love to make a difference.
I am grateful that Al was wearing that button that day
and willing to share his story.
I am grateful that there are families like this
who refuse to allow difference to destroy their love;
who are courageous enough to love even in the losing;
who speak with pride about their son—
a son some parents would want to hide because of
his orientation and the disease which claimed his life.
They were proud of their son, for in his dying he brought people
to a new awareness of a terrible disease.
In his dying, he brought people to a new level of compassion.
They were proud because their son's life had meaning.

■

We are so afraid of death.
But even more, we are afraid that we will die
and our lives will leave no mark.
We want to know when we breathe our last;
when we whisper those words,
"It is finished,"
that in those words another might find a new beginning.

■

We take our time at this station and recall another story.
The only sounds I heard
were the sounds of tears
muffled by the shoulder of a lover,

a brother, a mother, a friend.
Feet shuffling ever so slowly.
Stopping. Eyes gazing, recognizing a name, a face.
As soon as I walked into the auditorium,
I was struck by the memory of visiting the memorial at Dachau.
How quiet it was there.
How quiet it is here.
How so many people could make so little noise.
Stunned silence. The silence of memory.
Only tears and prayers have active voice.
All else must be silent.
Hundreds of people milling about, tracing the fabric
of the names stitched or written on Quilt panels.
Reading silently. Remembering. Names unknown.
Designs, pictures, drawings, words
that captured the identity of the one no longer with us.
At least not in person. But certainly in spirit.
Most certainly in memory.
Names unknown from places never visited
yet they share a common place.
A common cause of death.
A cause of death that has become all too common.
Dates of birth and dates of death.
All, each one, so young.
Parents clinging to each other.
They release their embrace long enough for her
to take a picture of the Quilt bearing her son's name.
The Quilt they made to remember him.
The camera clicks, flashes, and the memory is etched on film.
And heart.
Broken.
Poems. Lyrics from favorite songs.

Words that somewhere else would seem trite or shallow.
But not here. These were words written by heart not hand.
Faces depicting happier days when death was so distant
but came too soon. Much too soon.
There were some smiles, too.
Gentle, tender smiles.
Memories bring not only tears but smiles.
Remember how he could dance.
Remember his charm, his look.
Remember his passions. Remember his love.
Who were all these people whose names
are now forever stitched upon the Quilt?
The Names Quilt that continues to expand,
day by day,
city after city,
with no end in sight.
Standing, looking, reading, weeping.
An older man in a wheelchair held his granddaughter on his lap.
Her uncle's name was here. His son.
He sat there looking and drying his tears with a handkerchief.
I looked at each quilt panel, searching for his name.
I heard his name over the loudspeaker.
The litany of names.
Fr. Gary Jarvis.
But his panel wasn't on the main floor
or hanging from the balcony.
I went to the information table and asked.
"It's hanging in the foyer with the quilts that are new,"
the young man said.
Then I saw it.
The name. The dates. The words. The symbols.
For a brief moment I felt pride in our community.

The risk of putting our name with his.
Committing our name to fabric if not stone
and saying we stand in solidarity with those who have AIDS.
But this was no time for pride.
Only prayer.
Prayer for the dead.
Prayer for the living.
Prayer for understanding.
Prayer for a cure.
Prayer for a man whose name lives on in the minds and hearts
of those he touched.
And prayer that as we remember him in this small way,
he will remember us.
His memory gives us courage.
His name on the Quilt helps us to recommit ourselves
and redouble our efforts to include all,
especially those we have pushed away from our lives
because of our ignorance and our fear.
These names will live on.
That is what we have: their names.
And the memories.
The Quilt invites us to put our mouths around their names.
Say each one slowly,
prayerfully.
Let the name settle in our souls.
Let the images remind us of times of life, not death,
because we know this friend's life had meaning.

■

Standing by the cross of Jesus
are his mother and the beloved disciple, John,
the two people he wanted closest to him when he died.

They stayed with him all the way to the cross.
In his dying, Jesus brought them even closer together.
These two people, Mary and John,
reflect how Jesus brought the world near
through the blood he poured out on his cross.
He brought people not only a new awareness
and a new level of compassion;
Jesus brought people new life.
At this station,
we savor the taste of this sour wine upon our lips.
We don't spit it out.
For this common wine will be flavored with an uncommon
ingredient that will give our lives meaning.

PRAYER

We long for you, O God.
Like a deer yearns for running streams,
so our souls thirst for you.
May our lives drink in the sweet wine of your compassion.
May we taste again the uncommon vintage of our liberation.
May our souls find refreshment in the final words of your Son:
"It is finished."
These words refresh our souls because we know
they offer us a new beginning.
Deep down, O God,
we realize the wine of this world
will never be able to quench our thirst.
So we turn to you now with our parched, dry throats,
and ask only that you give us a sip of your kindness;
a taste of your compassion.
With this love upon our lips,
we kiss your cross and find meaning even in our pain.

Our lives do matter, O God,
when they are united with the death of your Son.
For in this cup of suffering
are mingled all our tears and all our fears.
Help us to pass this cup around.

THE THIRTEENTH STATION: PALL BEARERS
Jesus is taken down from the cross

I recall a friend telling me that one day he was visiting a friend of
his who was dying of cancer.
His friend told him,
"George, we have been friends for a long time.
But if you ever come to visit and feel sorry for me,
then I don't want you to come back."
Feeling sorry for another's plight is pity not compassion.
Commiseration is different from compassion.
Shared misery is different from shared suffering.
Pity puts the healthy one in a stance of looking down
upon the sick one.
Compassion places them side-by-side.
George's sick friend had reached an inner peace
that afforded him the courage to live and the courage to die.
He had found that the only healing possible in this world
of medical miracles is the ability to accept one's death
even as one fights to hang on to life.
With this healing comes abundant hope.
With this attitude, in the absence of a cure, comes compassion.
With this inner peace comes resurrection.
When his friend died, George was there,
holding on to his friend
for dear life.
At his friend's funeral, George was there,
a pall bearer
of life.

■

What causes us to live hidden lives?
What motivates us to keep our faith hidden from view of others?
Fear.
As John relates, after Jesus dies
"Joseph of Arimathea, a disciple of Jesus
(although a secret one because of fear),
asked Pilate's permission to remove Jesus' body." [John 19:38]
Joseph kept his faith hidden from others because he was afraid
of what others might say or do.
After all, he saw what happened to the one he secretly followed.
Another one of the pall bearers John mentions in his Gospel
is also a closet believer.
"Nicodemus (the man who had first come to Jesus at night)
likewise came, bringing a mixture of myrrh and aloes
which weighed about a hundred pounds." [19:39]
It was a heavy load for Nicodemus to carry,
but not as heavy as holding his secret belief in Jesus.
Before this, he was unsure because he sought out Jesus at night
when no one could see him.
But now he was certain.
Both he and Joseph stepped out into the light
as "they took Jesus' body" down from the cross,
and "in accordance with Jewish burial custom bound it up
in wrappings of cloth with perfumed oils." [v.40]

■

Fear may hold us prisoner for a while,
but it need not hold our faith hostage.
Take Alfred, for instance. He was a man of few words.
A shy man, Alfred lived his life without much fanfare

or fireworks. His co-workers admired his competence,
his diligent attitude toward his job.
They did not think of him as unfriendly or uncaring or unkind.
Alfred wasn't aloof or arrogant. He was just quiet. Steady.
A silent river that ran deep, sometimes blue, but always true.
Every night after work, Alfred stopped at Mrs. Cannali's house.
She was an 80-year-old woman who lived in the apartment
building down the street from Alfred. Sometimes he brought her
groceries or the newspaper or something from the store she had
asked for the night before.
Mainly Alfred just checked in to see if she was okay.
Every Saturday morning, Alfred visited the jail.
He listened to the prisoners, spent some time with them,
prayed with those who asked him to.
Every other Sunday, he went with members of his parish
to serve soup at the community kitchen for the poor
and homeless. And once a week, Alfred would call on Jimmy,
the little boy he had become a big brother for
a couple years ago. He'd take Jim bowling or to a movie or
to a ballgame or the mall. And they'd talk.
Alfred was a quiet man. A man of few words.
He is one of those great ones among us that we probably don't
know because often the greatest among us are the ones who
serve without expecting or desiring
recognition from the rest of us.
The greatest among us have no need to tell others what they do,
they just do it.
Like George and his friend,
like Joseph of Arimathea and Nicodemus,
Alfred was great because he was so small.
Though Alfred lived in the shadows,
his faith brought light to others.

He was great because he was concerned with the welfare of
others and showed his concern without expecting anything in
return.
It was a natural part of his day, his week, his life.
It was commonplace, natural.
If you knew Alfred and asked him how he found the time to do
so much, he would arch his eyebrow as if to say,
"What's the big deal?
Doesn't everyone do little things just as he did?"

■

Actions speak louder than attitudes;
witness is more compelling than words.
Each day of our lives we give a homily by the way we live,
the way we move,
the way we are with one another.
Each day we give a sermon on various themes:
from service to selfishness;
from hope and hospitality to indifference and impatience.
I guess Alfred knew the truth of what the prophets, like Isaiah,
and the suffering servant, Jesus, talked about when they put
words to their witness:
that when the gates of heaven swing open,
God is going to ask us only this:
How are the widow, the wronged, the wounded?
How are the orphans, the outcasts, the alienated?
How are the lonely, the lost, the unloved?
God will ask us the question that must have been stalking
both Joseph of Arimathea and Nicodemus.
The question that pushed them out of the night
and into the light:
"Have you taken my Son down from the cross yet?"

Joseph and Nicodemus: pall bearers for the body of Christ.
This is the stop along the way that reminds us that
now is the time to live those questions we've been
too frightened to face into answers.
With bold deeds, not words.
With exclamation points, not excuses.
With open hands, not closed hearts.
With faith, not fear.

PRAYER

When a bereaved widow asks us to be a pall bearer
for her husband's funeral,
we are honored to hold the body of our friend one last time.
This is not dead weight but the weight of all the memories,
all the stories,
all the glory we have shared through the years.
He's not heavy, he's holy.
Light as a feather floating in a gentle breeze.
When a grieving mother holds the lifeless body of her son,
we stay at a distance and reverence the moment.
But when the time is right, we move closer.
And when she is ready to let go of the body,
we gently take him from her arms.
Mary must have been grateful that these two men,
Joseph of Arimathea and Nicodemus, came out of hiding
long enough to find her son.
After the brave women who had been there all along
washed the blood from the body of Jesus,
these men wrapped his body with linen scented with myrrh.
What a memory this must have been for Mary.
The smell of happier times. The smell of new birth.
For this was one of the gifts brought to her son

soon after he was born.
And now it is being used to prepare her son's body for burial.
Give us the courage, O God,
to come out of the closets of our fear.
Even as our names go unmentioned,
may our actions speak with love and compassion
for those who are in need.
Even if our faces go unnoticed,
may our witness help others to hold the body of Christ
in their arms.
As you inspired Joseph and Nicodemus
to carry the body of Jesus
to its not-so-final resting place,
may you inspire us to carry on.

THE FOURTEENTH STATION: TOMB
Jesus is placed in the tomb

*In the place where he had been crucified
there was a garden,
and in the garden a new tomb
in which no one had ever been buried.
Because of the Jewish Preparation Day
they buried Jesus there,
for the tomb was close at hand. [John 19:41-42]*
Our journey takes us to a garden.
Not the Garden of Eden but the Garden of Endings.
A cemetery.
When my brother died, we buried him in the family plot
at St. Mary's Cemetery, near Lambert Field in St. Louis.
As we commended his body to the earth,
the planes taking off overhead caused a great distraction.
As I stopped the prayers of commendation to allow the roar
of the jet engines to fade in the distance,
I remember thinking:
I wonder if those people in the planes can see us.
I wonder if they can see this small group of people crowded
around an open grave that is about to be filled
with the body of my brother.

■

Our vantage point for this station, as with all the rest,
is not from above but from below.

We stand again on holy ground.
Cemeteries are holy places precisely because this ground
has been blessed by the body of Christ
who spent three days under it.
Like a seed planted in fertile soil,
we believe this body will rise again.
Cemeteries are quiet places, sacred spaces,
that move us to memory.
When we hear of someone going into a cemetery under the
cloak of darkness and defacing the tombstones, we name it for
what it is: desecration.
Amid all the devastation caused by the summer floods in 1993,
all the stories of people losing lives, homes, property, and
dreams, one of the most poignant reports was from the tiny town
of Hardin, MO, where the flood raged through the community's
cemetery and washed away hundreds of caskets. It took months
to retrieve them, and some were never recovered. Even among
those that were found, some could not be identified, and so the
people of Hardin had to dig a common grave
to hold the wet bones of their ancestors and loved ones.
At the ceremony that recommitted these bones to the earth,
the pain of this loss was etched on every face and carried in
every sentence of those who spoke to television reporters.
I remember one saying,
"The flood not only took away our present and our future,
it also took away our past."

■

And so we stand on this sacred ground
and remember the one we love who has died.
But as we stand here,
we also believe that the vision of Ezekiel will come true:

Thus says the Lord God to these bones: See!
I will bring spirit into you, that you may come to life...
O my people, I will open your graves and have you rise from
them, and bring you back to the land of Israel.
Then you shall know that I am the Lord,
when I open your graves and have you rise from them, O my
people! I will put my spirit in you that you may live,
and I will settle you upon your land. [Ezekiel 37:5,12-14]
Like these dry bones Ezekiel saw scattered upon the ground,
we are out of breath and seemingly out of time.
We long for this breath to stir upon the land of our hearts
to resuscitate us, for this death of the one we love
has knocked the wind out of us.
We sit now, doubled over,
and stare at the grave of the one we love.
Suddenly, we remember how "Mary Magdalene and the other
Mary remained sitting there, facing the tomb."
These are some well-worn words from the passion account
we hear as if for the first time.
"Facing the tomb" is what we do at this station.
Face the tomb where fear and death hide inside.
Face the tomb where neglect and indifference cling to the stone.
Face the tomb where anxiety and anguish climb the walls.
We stare at the tomb as one might stare at a face in the crowd
trying to memorize the features.
We stare at the tomb, we stare at his face,
and we don't recognize him.
Later, though, Mary will look at this one she knew and loved
and will say,
"I didn't recognize your voice."
Like a phone call from a long-forgotten friend,
we don't recognize the voice until we are called by name.

■

As I stood at my brother's grave that day we buried him,
I wanted to stay and just stare.
I wanted us to lower his body into the ground
rather than allow strangers to do it.
At the very least, I wanted each of us to throw
some sacred earth upon his body to somehow
bring closure to this moment of our greatest grief.
But after the holy water was sprinkled
and all the prayers were said,
we walked away.
And after we were in our cars to drive away,
I looked out the window and saw the cemetery workers
begin to lower Ed's body into the grave.
A plane roared overhead.
Was anybody watching from up in the skies?
Was anybody wondering who it was that had died?

PRAYER

We watch. We wait. We wonder. We pray.
We stay a while longer and just stare.
We face this tomb, so close at hand.
No roar from the heavens will distract us now.
Instead, we sense the earth moving beneath our feet.
We hear a groaning, a moaning.
The earth cannot hold this body much longer.
These bones, this body,
will rise again.
And as we hear the earth groan,
we listen for the sound of our name.

THE FIFTEENTH STATION: LIFE
Jesus is raised to new life

At the funeral of Arthur Ashe,
tennis star and human rights activist,
Andrew Young said that when he heard about Arthur's death,
he called Ashe's home to offer sympathy to the family.
What he heard was Arthur's voice on the answering machine:
"If you leave a message, I'll get right back to you."
That message on the answering machine offers
an image about death and life:
when one is passionate about truth and life,
justice and peace,
dignity and dreams,
one will leave a legacy that death will not conquer.
This is the message Jesus left us when he died:
"I'll get back to you."

■

"Why do you search for the Living One among the dead?"
the angels asked the women who had come at dawn
that first day of the week to pay their respects
at the tomb of their Teacher.
He is not here; he has been raised up.
Remember what he said to you while he was still in Galilee—that
the Son of God must be delivered into the hands
of sinful people, be crucified, and on the third day rise again.
[Luke 24:5-7]

These women checked the answering machines
in their minds and hearts and the Gospel reports
"his words came back to them." [v.8]
But when these women went back to tell the others
this astounding, amazing news,
"the story seemed like nonsense
and they refused to believe them." [Luke 24:11]
That's the way it often is with good news, isn't it?
We say, "It's too good to be true!"
Like the disciples huddled in that upper room,
we have to check this out for ourselves.
Like Thomas, we have to see it to believe it.
"It seemed like nonsense."
It doesn't make any sense.
How can a person who has died now be alive?
How can a person who has been crucified now be among the
living? How can a body that has been buried in a tomb now be
breathing? It doesn't make any sense!
But if it doesn't,
then this whole sojourn of the soul has not made any sense.
Does it make any sense that people should live in poverty
in the wealthiest country on the planet?
Does it make any sense that people should sleep in the street
when vacant buildings are demolished?
Does it make any sense to us that children can no longer play
safely in their own yards for fear that someone might drive by
and shoot them or snatch them away?
Does it make any sense that children die of hunger
while food is thrown away?
Does it make any sense that some elderly people have to lead
lives of quiet desperation and lingering loneliness
because they have outlived their friends

and their families forget to visit?
Does it make any sense that people take grudges to their graves,
refusing to forgive an injury that may have happened
so long ago they can not even remember the circumstances
that caused their pain?
Does it make any sense that we kill people
to show people that killing people is wrong?
Does it make any sense that we sometimes go to war to make
peace? Does it make any sense that babies are aborted
while parents unable to have any children wait to adopt?
Does any of this make sense?
Yet we don't say, "the story seems like nonsense,"
because we have just grown so accustomed to the face of death.
If this sojourn of the soul has made any sense at all,
it is that we have tried to walk with,
stand with,
and weep with those for whom the way of the cross
is not a Lenten devotional but a daily grind.
And this walk through the valley of tears and fears
would not make any sense at all
if not for this final stop along the way.
If the empty tomb doesn't make any sense to us,
then we are people of death, not life.
If the resurrection of Jesus doesn't knock some new sense
into our heads and hearts,
then we have walked this way with our eyes closed.
If we continue to accept the death,
the injustice,
the oppression,
the poverty,
the hunger,
the homelessness,

the violence
we see or read about or experience each day
as simply the way of the world,
"the way it is,"
then this walk of the cross has been a waste of time.
And the empty tomb will seem like nonsense.

■

But the way of death is not the way it is.
No, through this journey Jesus has shown us a new way.
And at this station,
the empty tomb,
the last on our journey but the first of a new way of living,
we hear the message:
"Accept no limitations!"
That is the message Jesus has recorded on the human heart:
do not limit your possibilities;
do not limit your love,
your compassion,
your passion for peace
and for life.
Do not accept the limitations of the tomb!
Enlarge your hearts,
your minds,
your souls!
And remember:
"I'll get back to you."

■

That is why we have made this trip:
to learn how to live in the midst of death

by following in the footsteps of Jesus,
the author of all life.
We stand now before the empty tomb
and know that trip was worth the trouble.
Because now, like the first disciple who went racing to that tomb
after the women had told their story,
"we see and we believe."
We see the empty tomb and we believe.
We see the wounds on the resurrected body of Christ
and we believe.
We see the scars on each other's hearts and we believe.
Seeing and believing,
we know that Christ has died
and so we commit ourselves to walk this way of compassion.
We know that Christ has risen
and so commit ourselves to live this truth that sets us free.
We know that Christ will come again
and so commit ourselves to live the message Jesus
has recorded on our very human yet very holy hearts:
"I'll get back to you."

PRAYER

O God of Life,
we have arrived at that place where,
in the words of the Zen monk, Mamon Ekai,
"the great path has no gates
and thousands of roads enter it.
When one passes through this gateless gate,
one walks freely between heaven and earth."
We rejoice in your gift of Life, O God.
Your Son, Jesus,
the Way, the Truth, and the Life,

has set us free to follow a new way
of living, loving, and forgiving.
Continue to inspire us along this road of compassion,
this avenue of adventure,
this highway of holiness.
Help us to see,
to believe,
and to live the truth
that the empty tomb means eternal life.
With this message etched upon our memories,
may we bring this life to all we meet along the way.
May we and all your peoples walk
"freely between heaven and earth."